It's Not All In Your Head

by Vicki Hart

WHAT READERS ARE SAYING...

"Life as a pastor's wife can be a wonderful blessing, but there are unique challenges, stressors, and temptations in ministry. A caring pastor may inadvertently create an environment that invites various attraction levels from women besides his wife. Where can a pastor's wife share her concerns when she feels strange about overly friendly females in the church or an overly receptive husband in the pulpit? She may think it's all in her head. Her irritation, suspicions, or fears may be minimized or dismissed. Too many marriages, families, and churches become collateral damage after unhealthy attention leads to insecurity, lack of boundaries, inappropriate attachments, and devastating affairs. In this honest and hopeful book, Vicki Hart shares her painful journey and wise insights to help other ministry couples recognize, avoid, and heal from improper female attention towards male pastors."

Linda Kline
Pastoral Director
Psalm One Ministries
www.psalmone.org

Psalm One provides Soul care, Sabbath getaways, and encouragement for those in ministry as well as anyone hungry for greater intimacy in their walk with God. Bible teaching and Christ-centered spiritual formation on-site near Cincinnati, and off-site around the U.S. and around the world. In addition, Linda does retreats, seminars, counseling and consulting specifically for pastors, pastors' wives, and adult children of pastors affected by life in the church.

Linda Kline, a native of Louisville, Kentucky, is a former staff member of Cru and a graduate of Trinity Evangelical Divinity School in Deerfield, Illinois. She teaches the Bible and Christ-centered spiritual formation around the US and around the world. She facilitates soul care, Sabbath renewal, and spiritual growth through various retreats and gatherings for men and women. She counsels, consults, and serves on the Steering Committee of the Caregivers Forum, an international network which supports, equips, and strengthens those on the front lines of ministry.

—————————

"*It's Not All in Your Head* explores the problem of transference in the church, which can occur when women become infatuated with their pastors. As the director of a ministry for pastor's wives for over twenty years, I can confirm that this is still a major problem in congregations today. Author Vicki Hart knows the devastating effect transference can have in ministry and courageously shares her personal experience to shed light on a taboo subject. Towards the end, her husband, George, writes a chapter. Getting a little male perspective provides balance, which lets women know that any uncomfortable feelings they have should be validated. In other words, it's not all in their heads."

Jannice May
Founder and Director
Connecting and Bonding Ministry
Connects the minister's wives and bonds friendships forever.
www.connectingandbonding.org

Jannice May is the founder and president of Connecting and Bonding Inc., an organization serving ministers' wives. Jannice's passion for this ministry stems from having served in full-time pastoral ministry with her husband Curtis for 39 years. During that time, she noticed ministers' wives had no resources to help them be supportive of their husbands without losing their own identity.

When asked for help from a young minister's wife, she realized there needed to be a way for them to be mentored and encouraged by other ministers' wives. Plus, they needed a safe environment where they could share their struggles and concerns. So her Connecting and Bonding Ministry was born and is still going strong after 22 years.

Jannice and Curtis have been married for 53 years and have served in various ministries all over the United States. They presently reside in California. Their two married children and spouses, plus their two grandchildren, bring them an abundance of joy.

Contents

CHAPTER 1
IT'S NOT ALL IN YOUR HEAD

INFIDELITY AND THE NUMBER OF AFFAIRS is at an all-time high. Unfortunately, the church is not immune and the number of male pastors having affairs with a female member of the congregation is staggering. Statistics from several sources including: Standing Stone; a ministry shepherding shepherds cites 40% (if you count an emotional as well as a literal affair). The actual number may be even higher as many go unreported. Transference is a huge contributor to infidelity among pastors and can be a steppingstone to an affair.

As a spouse of a former pastor of over thirty years, I intend to bring insight and awareness of what transference is. I also intend to address why pastors are so susceptible, and how the church can be a perfect setting for transference to occur. Insight and understanding produces greater awareness and prevention; whereby lives, marriages, careers, and churches can be spared the devastation that an affair can bring. I choose to convey a message of hope to pastoral couples and the church in this area.

The title of this book was chosen to validate the women whose voices expressed their concern or intuition over something or someone but it has been ignored; especially spouses of pastors. Transference is a little understood and huge issue within the church. My prayer is that this book would become a part of the solution to this crisis within the body of Christ.

Chapter 2
What is Transference?

A s previously stated, statistics within the church are quite alarming in regard to the staggering number of male pastors who have an emotional or literal affair with a member of the congregation.

The church remains silent on this topic, that is until a catastrophe occurs. Disciplinary action is usually taken with little to no discussion or follow-up. The definition of **transference** is, "a psychological bond between people in which one person's reaction in a current relationship is influenced by his/her former relationship patterns to significant persons rather than by the stimuli present in the context of the current relationship." This may occur wherever interpersonal relationships are present, and they are always irrational or inappropriate responses. They may either be positive or negative, and can carry both positive and negative implications at the same time. The threats of transferential distortions are not to be denied. They are complex and powerful.

Pastors receive limited, if any preparation or instruction regarding transference issues. They are rarely prepared to appropriately deal with this phenomenon and are not shown how to insulate themselves against the constant affection of females in the flock by setting healthy boundaries. As a spouse of a former full-time pastor, as well as having many friendships with spouses of pastors, I know first-hand that this is a serious issue within the church. By bringing awareness, I hope to also bring instruction, preparedness, openness, discussion, and prevention regarding this issue. My desire is to circumvent the serious consequences that transference issues cause for pastors, their families and their congregations.

Understanding transference should definitely be included as part of every pastor's training. I know of no other issue that has caused as much havoc and pain among pastors, families and congregations within the body of Christ. Again, it is only when a situation of serious consequence occurs that the matter is usually addressed with disciplinary action, but it is not discussed openly for various ethical reasons.

The particular facet of transference that I am addressing in this book is female transference to a male pastor. I understand that transference can also involve male to male or female to female, but my story will involve the issue of female attraction or an extremely unhealthy emotional attachment/obsession toward a male pastor on the part of females within the congregation. I know from my own personal experience and discussion with other pastor's wives that this is a common occurrence within the church. Some pastor's wives have assured me they have a handle on this complex issue by merely monitoring their husbands, keeping track of his calls and emails, and one even told me that the solution for her was to stand right next to her husband at church every week. One pastor's wife said that she wasn't that concerned, now that her husband had shown signs of aging; like balding and a large middle section, as if that would keep the women at bay, but don't be so secure. Solutions for this matter are not quite that simple.

Immediately upon my husband's entry into the role of "Pastor," I noticed the astonishing amount of female attention directed toward him. Most of it was harmless. Women love to dote on their pastor, by doing small innocent things like, bringing his favorite dish to the potluck and making sure he gets to sample it. Should he mention something that he likes; such as a certain picture perhaps, it will usually show up as a gift on Pastor Appreciation Day, usually purchased by a woman in the congregation. In one congregation, my husband mentioned that he loved deviled eggs. So, one lady started making him deviled eggs on a regular basis. I jokingly used to say, "Honey, those are the devil's eggs, all right." Now, I think it would be interesting what her reaction might have been had I brought her husband's favorite dish for him every week. I seriously doubt it would have been warmly received, but again because he was her pastor, it was somehow accepted. So I just put on my pastor's wife smile and dealt with it since it's pretty typical for a pastor to be shown special affection by most of the females in the congregation. I may not have particularly liked it, but I could live with it because I understood that people tend to love their pastor.

One lady in one of our congregations, would make a bee line for George for her weekly pastor hug when he walked in the door. I want to mention that this woman was greatly endowed in a certain area and quite tall. Visualize for a moment based on these descriptions: since she was quite a bit taller than he was, his face was strategically placed in an awkward position when she went in for her hug. She would come close to squeezing the life out of him and he would laugh on our way home that he had to come up for air. Ok, I think you get the point, so we'll move on from that.

But often it becomes more serious and goes a bit further and deeper. It can begin to take on a whole new dimension where women begin to idealize and target their affections on their pastor, who they perceive to be greater than he actually is. They can begin to idolize him, set their affection upon him, and strive for his attention. The spouse of the pastor can be seen as an obstacle preventing them from getting closer to the pastor. This can make her a target of malice and gossip. As in classic transference cases, when the affection ceases or the pastor no longer meets their expectations, the mood shifts and it can be taken as a form of rejection, suddenly turning from idealization to disdain or intense anger. This usually results in an agenda of discrediting the pastor, spreading vicious rumors, or questioning his character to others who will listen. Sowing discord would be a good description of this occurrence.

Chapter 3
Why Pastors?

R ESEARCH AND MY OWN EXPERIENCE indicate that there's several reasons why pastors are often targets of transference. I want to reiterate here that Transference is a *psychological bond between people in which one person's reaction in a current relationship is influenced by his/her former relationship patterns to significant persons rather than by the stimuli present in the context of the current relationship.* This means that in this particular instance It's the redirection of the woman's feelings for a past significant person to the pastor. This transference is often manifested as an erotic attraction towards the pastor, but can be seen in many other forms such as rage, hatred, mistrust, , extreme dependence, or even placing the pastor in a god-like or guru status.

Pastors are in a position of authority and are considered a representative of God. I cannot begin to tell you the amount of times a lady in our congregation would say with stars in her eyes, how wonderful it must be to be married to my husband. This is the phenomenon of idealization, an exaggerated attachment to or interpretation or valuing of another. Respect for the office is one thing, but idealizing and putting someone on a pedestal is quite another. I sometimes wanted to respond that they had not seen how grumpy he had been that week, how he left the toilet seat a mess, and didn't pick up his underwear or socks, but I didn't. I would most often just put on my sweet smile and refrain from the comments I really wanted to express. My sister-in-law, who is also the spouse of a pastor had the perfect response when that occurred with ladies in her congregation. In her sweet, South Carolina accent, she would reply, "Well, he's really not all that." You can get away with quite a bit with a southern accent.

The few times I did decide to share some frustration or honesty about my husband, it was met with a look of shock. Now they could share frustrations from home about their husband with no repercussions but if I did so, I usually found it dismissed as my problem and invariably they would come to his defense. Now, my husband is a fine man but let's face it, he is a man and he has his flaws.

Therapists are trained to recognize transference; pastors generally are not. Relatively little work has been done in this area within the church. Dr. Frank Lake, a British psychiatrist worked extensively in this area in the Anglican Church. He provides resources to deal with the subject of "transference in the church." Dr. Archibald Hart, a licensed psychologist, has also written articles regarding the dangers of transference in the church, but there is a huge gap between some of this information and the training of future pastors. Evangelicals, seemingly choose to simply avoid the problem altogether.

If a pastor does his job well, then transference in

pastoral care is going to occur. Whenever someone is met with kindness and compassion from someone in a position of authority, the opportunity exists for transference to happen. Pastors are very susceptible for many reasons, some of which are listed below. It's not a question of whether or not it will happen, but rather will it be recognized and wisely handled when it does?

- Pastors are in a position of authority and much of the pastor's job involves listening, showing empathy and compassion. All of these create a powerful emotional connection.

- The pastor is easily accessible and available to the congregation. There are typically no red flags when a woman parishioner calls, texts, or emails the pastor. However, if I (as a woman) were to call someone's husband to talk about any matter, red warning flags would go up immediately. Even, in the best of friendships this would or should cause alarm. My husband has had calls from women late at night, while on vacation, and all hours of the day. The calls many times involved church related issues which would then turn into conversations about life. I recently found out that one particular lady in our congregation was calling him several times a week and talking sometimes up to 45 minutes on a call.

- Pastors are up in front every week delivering messages which are taken as direct messages from God. Every week they bare their soul, which can be a very attractive attribute; therefore creating unhealthy connections. When a pastor exhibits confidence and passion on stage, there are those who find this very attractive. There is a false perception that this person is far above everyone else in the spiritual realm and that they have a direct line to God, unlike anyone else.

- Pastors are considered safe confidants and many times the first point of contact when there is a problem. The pastor is someone that most women perceive as a safe place to share their innermost concerns or secrets. Many times those secrets have never been shared with anyone else, not even their husband or close family members. Women are usually the first to come forward with problems within their marriage. They may share these sometimes sensitive and very intimate details with their pastor. Women have shared their lack of love for their spouse, molestation issues, abortions and very intimate issues of their past with my husband. This creates an intimacy and connection that can become very unhealthy.

- Pastors are the first ones to be called and they're often present in someone's greatest time of grief or sorrow when situations such as sickness, death of a spouse, or other family member or friend occur. They are also the first ones called at times of great celebration such as a birth, wedding, baptism, or ordination. These are times of great emotion and increased vulnerability for unhealthy emotional connections.

- Pastors are involved in conjoint volunteer activities, including mission trips and travel opportunities outside the confines of the church setting. Sometimes pastors will say that if they counsel a woman alone in their office, they keep the door open or have a window in their office. While this is a good practice, an office visit isn't typically where emotional attachments occur. In fact, this would probably be one of the last places that an emotional attachment would occur. In a counseling or therapy situation the setting is an office, and yes it still happens, but the church setting provides countless additional opportunities for unhealthy attachments to develop.

- The pastor in a small church is the center of

it all. In our last congregation there was far too much focus on my husband's warmth and personality. I brought this concern to our leadership team several times but to no avail. If the pastor exhibits a warm, outgoing personality, women can be particularly drawn to them, especially if the woman is married to an extremely low-key, introverted, background type of man. Even very introverted pastors display extra warmth and energy while they are on the job at church.

- There is also something appealing to the male ego that relishes the thought of rescuing the "damsel in distress." The pastor may feel like the hero rescuing a woman in need. They have the best of intentions but can get sucked in over their head before they realize what is happening. Pastors need to recognize their limitations, learn when and who to refer to when issues get deeper than they are trained or equipped to handle. Since their counseling training is usually very limited, this should be almost immediately after the issue is brought to them. There are huge risks involved by not doing so.

Regarding this issue on a personal note, there was a young lady who had some serious mental health issues, one of them being an eating disorder. She moved out of state and would call my husband on a regular basis. She would keep him on the phone for more than an hour each time. My concern deepened, so I called my son-in-law who has a Masters in Counseling and was working in the mental health field. He assured me that my concerns were valid and that George was in over his head. Because of her fragile emotional state, George feared refusing her calls so, we compromised by agreeing that I would be present during the call and that he would let her know this up front. Once I started joining in on the call, the length of her calls diminished greatly and soon they ceased altogether.

- Men in general, tend to enjoy female attention. In a healthy situation and with good boundaries, interchange between male and female can be very enjoyable and insightful. Studies reveal that the most beautiful sound to a male infant is the sound of a woman's voice. There is certainly nothing wrong with that. But we don't live in a perfect world and we are broken in areas and ways we do not even realize. The pastor may be especially vulnerable to female attention during particular seasons. For instance, during times of boredom (remember David in the Bible);

times of stress in a marriage; like the birth of a child or illness, during intense emotional stress like a death of a parent, or intense busy schedules, and times of life transitions. There is also the problem of countertransference, where the pastor's own unresolved past issues have not been dealt with and he is especially vulnerable.

- We often let our guard down in the church because we consider ourselves one big family. Community can be a very good thing, but all that glitters is not gold. We should constantly be vigilant because Satan and his cohorts are also faithful in coming to church. In fact, they may be much more faithful than most of the members. They show up at everything, seeking who they may devour. And it's usually the pastor or their spouse they would most like to devour.

To be fair, I believe that most women do not intend to get emotionally involved with a pastor. The church however, can offer the perfect setting for this to occur. One important point to consider is that when you observe the pastor, he is at his best because he's on the job. Most women don't typically see their husbands at his job where he is operating at his best. They see him in the evening after he comes home, totally drained after a day's work.

So my point is this, women don't see the pastor when he comes home from his job, "the church" totally drained, sitting there with nothing left to give, only wanting to sit and indulge in mindless activities such as watching TV. So many women compare their husband to the pastor and their husband falls short; this could be one reason why.

Even though counselors and therapists are trained to recognize transference and are aware of the consequences such as loss of their license and livelihood; statistics from several sources show that a small percentage still have affairs with their clients. As stated previously, this percentage is much higher in the church.

To be fair, I don't deny that there are truly predatory pastors out there. That type of pastor seems to be getting a significant amount of focus and attention. I do not intend to minimize the pain inflicted on any woman nor the story she has, having been a victim of one of these kind of pastors. There are those men who use their power and authority to prey on women who are vulnerable, and this should be dealt with, but it's a separate topic for another day. I will again speak from my perspective as a spouse of a male pastor for over 34 years. My husband was not a predatory pastor but truly had a desire to serve God and those within the congregation. I don't personally know any predatory pastors either. The male pastors that I know and are familiar with, went into the pastorate calling with a deep desire to serve Christ and lead others to Him.

CHAPTER 4
THE AFFAIR
EMOTIONAL/LITERAL

INFIDELITY IS NOTHING TO PLAY AROUND WITH. It is the utmost form of both disrespect and insult to your spouse and to yourself. It can destroy you and your marriage. An emotional affair is not to be minimized, it can be equally as destructive as a literal affair. Not only is it the steppingstone to a literal affair, but it can create havoc all by itself within a marriage. At a retreat, a spouse of a pastor chided me when I shared my experience; as if my experience was far less traumatic than what her husband did to her by having a literal affair. But unhealthy attachments and emotional affairs are intensely destructive. Let's not minimize the effects of an emotional affair and we must stop minimizing one another's pain.

Far too many well-known Christian leaders who have had an affair will attest to the damage it can do. It can truly undo much good. Many names come to mind. Anyone who has ever watched the movie, "Fatal Attraction" with Michael Douglas and Glen Close cannot help but have the "heebie geebies" scared out of them about having an affair. I believe it would be wise to insist that watching this movie be a part of pastoral training.

An affair is defined as a sexual relationship, romantic friendship, or passionate attachment between two people without the attached person's significant other knowing. Through investing emotional energy and time with one another outside the marital relationship, the former platonic friendship can begin to form a strong emotional bond which hurts the intimacy of the spousal relationship. About half of such emotional involvements do eventually turn into full-blown affairs.

Douglas LaBier, Ph.D. writes in Psychology Today that there are six different kinds of affairs:

The "It's-Only-Lust" Affair

This is the most common and is mostly about sex. It can feel really intense, but it's also the quickest to flame out. An example is a person who's able to feel sexually alive and free only in a secret relationship, hidden from the imagined hovering, inhibiting eye of one's parent, which the person may experience unconsciously with his or her spouse.

The "I'll Show You" Affair

When a spouse is feeling unaffirmed, ignored and disregarded by their partner they can try to create a solution with an affair. Beneath this anger is a desire for someone who would really recognize him/her. This only leads to dealing with more trauma.

The "Just-In-The-Head" Affair

Two people find they have much in common, a similar outlook on life and spiritual compatibility as well. They enjoy talking and look forward to time together. They speak on the phone frequently and linger around to talk to each other. Soon a very intimate and emotionally close bond develops and it becomes much more than just a friendship. It's more of an affair of the mind and not the body but it's also more than just a friendship. Usually people in this kind of affair find something in each other that's lacking in their "real" relationship, and they're not dealing with that. Aside from the challenge of remaining on the chaste side of the sexual borderline, such "lovers" must hope that their primary partners continue to believe they're telling the truth. And there's a risk that what they're not finding in their primary relationship will become increasingly disruptive to it.

The "All-in-the-Family" Affair

This is usually considered fail-safe because no one will suspect it. This usually happens in an extended family situation where there are years of mutual, erotic teasing by relatives by marriage. The thought is that it will remain a secret, that neither will make any demands on the other and it would be perfectly safe. That is truly naïve thinking. Most "family" affairs are interwoven with family dysfunctions and buried resentments. The family affair can quickly turn into a family nightmare.

The "It's-Not-Really-An-Affair" Affair

Humans are experts at creating illusions for themselves. In this affair, one party is available but the other isn't. The available partner believes that the other really will leave his or her spouse if given enough time and patience. A relationship requires two equally available and committed people. Usually it's women who are caught in this trap, believing that their lovers will leave their spouses, but ninety percent of the time this never happens. Sometimes it comes out that they are just one of multiple affairs throughout the marriage.

The "Mind-Body" Affair

Here is the most dangerous for the lovers' existing relationships. It's so powerful because it feels so complete –emotionally, sexually, intellectually, and spiritually. They feel like "soul-mates." The "mind-body" affair is highly threatening to a marriage because it feels so "right." This kind of affair most frequently leads to divorce and remarriage. The upside is that the new relationship may prove to be the right match for the couple. Nevertheless, it generates all the mixed consequences that all affairs produce, especially when children are involved.

Stepping into any of these situations means that you're stepping into dangerous territory, especially as a pastor. Transference can be the point of entry. Instead of destroying your mate and your reputation with an affair, perhaps a better solution is to come clean and end it if a relationship is truly over on your part and can't be fixed.

CHAPTER 5
IT GETS PERSONAL

A NATIVE AMERICAN PROVERB SAYS, "Tell me the facts and I'll learn. Tell me the truth and I'll believe. But tell me a story and it will live in my heart forever." You can talk statistics and define terminology all day long, but there is no illustration quite so convincing as your own personal experience or story. At this season of my life, I personally have come to a place of healing and forgiveness to where I harbor no ill will towards anyone involved in my own particular situation. Since my husband's retirement from the pastorate, I am released from being a spouse of a pastor and let me state that it truly is a time of incredible freedom for both of us. I feel personally, that it is great to have my husband back. We are both continuing to be very active in ministry but we are once again George and Vicki and not Pastor George and "what's your name again." Thankfully, in this season of our marriage we are experiencing a new season of freedom, joy and wholeness.

Being the spouse of a pastor was only one facet of my life. I have worn many other hats such as daughter, realtor, office manager, paralegal, mom, grandmother, teacher and friend. Let me also state that there is no other career that directly involves the spouse and family as the pastorate does. It is a privilege to serve God in any capacity. However, sometimes burdens that others place on us and that we place on ourselves, are greater than God would ask of us. Jesus says in Matthew 11:30 (NIV) that His yoke is easy, and His burden is light. That is not the case in most churches today. I personally believe that the expectations and burdens that have been placed on the pastor, have far exceeded the expectations that God would place on any one man. Statistics and the burn out rate of pastors support my opinion. In the church the position has taken on a status which is not even biblical. "Pastor" is derived from the Latin word meaning shepherd. A shepherd is one who leads a flock to pasture for grazing. I personally, know a woman who leads a powerful ministry of caring for pastors, pastor's wives and families, who has stated that if a man isn't a narcissist when he goes into the pastorate, he may become one while in that role. We have put pastors on such a high pedestal and when you put anyone on a pedestal, they usually fall off.

I do not want to diminish or disrespect the office or the calling, but in my opinion, we have elevated the office within our present church culture far above what God would even desire. As in the days of Moses, the people wanted to hear from Moses and not God. I believe far too many Christians are pastor dependent rather than being God dependent. They rely on the pastor for their spiritual walk and sustenance for their journey. However, I want people to remember that the pastor is simply a shepherd to equip you and point you to God. They were not meant to be "God in the Flesh."

CHAPTER 6
OUR JOURNEY BEGINS

My HUSBAND AND I MET AND STARTED dating at a small Christian college in East Texas. I worked in the registrar's office so, I had access to his essay that he wrote for admission. In the essay he stated that he felt called to be a pastor. My jaw dropped when I saw that he felt called to serve in that role. Several of my friends had been Preacher Kids (PKs) and I had no desire to be the spouse of a pastor as I witnessed firsthand some of the difficulties this placed upon a family.

Growing up in a pastor-dependent, male dominant church; I witnessed such a strong focus on the pastor but his wife seemed to be invisible or at least unimportant, and assigned to mostly menial tasks. I told him that I did not want to be an invisible spouse. He assured me that he now felt that he should go into the business world, but yet serve in a local congregation. That arrangement suited me just fine. So, he graduated with a Business and Theology degree. After counsel and prayer, we decided to settle in Winston-Salem, North Carolina. The church we attended was quite large and welcomed our energy and zeal to serve. We both had extremely good jobs and were settling into marriage and life quite well.

I decided to be a stay at home mom when our son was born five years later. Two and a half years after that, our daughter was born. Following a couple of weeks after our daughter's birth and seven years into our marriage, the Assistant Pastor position in our congregation became available. My husband was quite successful in his corporate job and had been advancing rapidly. The Senior Pastor asked George if he would be interested in that position and whether he would consider working for less money and more hours. It was actually quite a bit less money, I might add. After prayer and discussion, we decided it was the path we were destined to take. I truly did not want to stand in the way of my husband's calling. Furthermore, I had made a promise to God when I was around 8 years old that I would do whatever he asked me to do. I remembered that prayer and moved forward in support of my husband. When I called my mother to tell her of our decision, she was not the least surprised and told me for the first time that even when I was a young child she knew I would marry a pastor.

I was 27 years young and very naïve in many ways when we entered into full-time ministry. Before the Associate Pastor left, he and my husband were standing together at a youth event when I observed that they were surrounded by an abundance of admiring females. His wife and I were standing close by when she said to me, "Welcome to the ministry. From now on, your husband is going to be admired by lots and lots of females. It just comes with the territory." She said that women were always telling her how wonderful and good looking her husband was. I thought she seemed a bit tainted, maybe even a bit angry, but now some 30 years later, I understand fully what she was talking about. I discovered early on that pastors were "babe magnets."

We embarked on our new chapter with gusto. After three years, we moved to Georgia where George pastored two congregations which were 100 miles from each other. Even though being a pastor was my husband's calling, I loved the Lord and jumped in to serve as well. I took on almost all of the tasks at home. Now thanks to Geri Scazzero, and her book, "I Quit" and renamed, "The Emotionally Healthy Woman," I realize that I over-functioned at home with free labor running the household and tending to the children so George could be about doing "the Lord's Work." You learn and you grow. Hindsight is always clearer.

After our year in Georgia, we moved to Birmingham, AL where he pastored two congregations which were sixty miles apart. Four years later, we moved to Buffalo, New York and he pastored a church there as well as one in Olean, sixty miles south, through the snow belt. Huge doctrinal changes in our denomination made my husband question whether or not he should stay in the ministry. He had a job offer which would result in a partnership in a very lucrative auto parts company outside of Birmingham. To determine our direction, I paid for him to attend the Pastor's Clergy Conference in Atlanta. Upon his return, he felt that he should stay in full-time ministry and also work in the area of racial diversity. While he was gone, I prayed and told God that I would go wherever he asked and make the most of it, but I reminded God that I had always wanted to go back to my home state of Ohio. A couple of months later, we received a call to move to Cincinnati and pastor two congregations there. One was predominately African American and the other Caucasian. Several years after our move, we merged them into one.

I must say that along the way we met a lot of wonderful people who became like family to us. Many of the people we stay in contact with to this day. I found it exciting and interesting to live and learn about the history of each area where we lived. I did miss being close to my own family of origin and this took its toll on my parents, especially my mom. She missed many years of being around her grandchildren. I simply was not able to get back for many family events like reunions, weddings and funerals. It was especially hard when I missed the funerals of three of my grandparents. Moving about every four years was a huge challenge. God provided the strength for the journey, but yet it was still difficult to keep uprooting our lives. I put my dreams and desires on the back burner again and again to support my husband's calling. Serving as a pastor was my husband's calling, not mine, yet his calling influenced my life in a huge way and many times kept me from fulfilling mine.

During all of our moves, one thing I could not help

but notice was that everywhere we served was lots of female attention directed towards my husband. Women doted over him by greeting with him in one congregation with a cup of coffee, as well as brownies or cookies. They would always have them ready for him as he entered the building. I felt a little like the unwanted step child. My mom asked one time when she was visiting where my treats were and we both just rolled our eyes and laughed. But after thirty years of this feeling, it wasn't quite so funny.

In one congregation, we were all set to take a trip with our teens out to Jackson Hole, Wyoming when right before our trip our son got a contagious virus. Because of this, I decided not to go and to take my two children up to Buffalo, New York. We were moving there in three weeks and had not found a home yet. While there, I did purchase a home which is another story in itself, but upon the church group's return, it was obvious that one woman had become especially fond of my husband. However, that didn't bother me too much because I knew we were leaving the state within the next few weeks.

My husband is a very open and gregarious personality. He is an ESFP, according to the Myers-Briggs Type Indicator, which is a very rare type to be in pastoral ministry. He is usually the life of the party and a natural born leader. In every church there was at least one woman that caused me some concern and wrote my husband what I called, "love notes" about how wonderful his sermons were and how his counseling had ministered to her so much. There were those women who always seemed available to do whatever needed to be done and to make sure it was done his way.

One woman in Alabama called him daily after her husband had an affair, until we both became extremely uncomfortable with her attachment to him. But we were young and somewhat naive. I know it is freeing to openly share and release some of our deepest secrets but frankly, I'm not sure a male pastor should be the one a female parishioner shares her most intimate secrets with. During our early years in ministry, I was still pretty involved in church activities. I was young and still pretty cute so I wasn't too concerned about most of the women or this particular issue yet. Our length of stay helped too because, as I became concerned about a particular woman we were off and running to our next location. My life became busier as I started working part time once our children started school. In addition to working I was running the household, raising my children, and furthering my education so a lot more of my time was diverted to other areas away from the church.

In New York, I worked as an office manager and legal assistant for an attorney in downtown Buffalo. He paid for my schooling as a paralegal so I could then write his pleadings and research the law, which I loved. I also handled all of his real estate and developed a strong interest in that area. After our move to Cincinnati, our family's financial needs were increasing as our children entered middle and high school. The financial pressure required me to go to work full time. I also desired my own challenge and opportunity to use my gifts and fulfill my calling. I never desired to be a mere extension of my husband as I have my own gift mix and personality. I knew that God ordained work for me to do on this earth. I decided to pursue one of my dreams and obtain my real estate license.

It was a perfect fit for me and my personality, with my business background and ability to work with various types of people. I had extremely keen insight on pricing, marketing, staging, and negotiation skills. I am a strong S/D on the DISC personality profile which has me described as a woman of steel and velvet. I was service and people oriented, and yet could be most direct or assertive when needed. You can't be a good realtor if you don't have a bit of firmness, mental toughness or decisiveness and the ability to confront.

My career began to take off when a top realtor noticed me as a rising star and offered me a full partnership. I accepted and our business skyrocketed, becoming extremely lucrative. I achieved many awards and received "Circle of Excellence" status consecutively for many years in a row. I was still involved in some ministry within the church but with a demanding career of my own, and two teens, my time spent within the church became somewhat limited.

I began to see that much of my ministry consisted of assisting people outside of the church through the stress of moving, purchasing their dream home, or selling and marketing their home to help them obtain the utmost value. A home purchase is the most single investment anyone will usually make and I had a passion for helping people in this area. It allowed us the ability to meet the demands of a growing family, pay off our mortgage, take some great vacations and assist our children with college and other amenities.

Upon our arrival in Cincinnati, I immediately had concerns about the attention one particular woman showed towards my husband. It was her body language, her attentiveness to him, and the observation that she would always go for the chair next to him. If we were in a group setting, she directed her full attention, eye contact and communication to him as though they were the only ones in the room. She liked to corner him after church and in small group meetings to ask various questions. As a woman, I felt uncomfortable with the attention she was showering on him, but mostly I felt uncomfortable with his obvious enjoyment of it. Immediately following his sermon, she would make a bee line to him to discuss and applaud his message. If he made a joke, she was the first one to laugh. She made many phone calls to him about various issues. She also couldn't seem to do enough for the church.

I sensed that she was extremely unhappy in her own marriage. I also sensed that things really began to escalate between her and my husband after a mission trip to New Orleans. It was a shared experience that she seemed to relish and a topic that came up often. Although I did help raise the funds, I did not attend the trip due to my job commitment. After her return, her attitude towards me seemed to change and I felt a bit of competition between us, maybe even jealousy would be a fit description. Now I will also mention that there was significant weight loss and some other work on her part as well which greatly improved her attractiveness. I believe she was enjoying her attractiveness and unfortunately, so was my husband. She was also several years younger than me. She had a seductive power over him that became very obvious to me. I sensed a strong emotional connection between them. He would follow her around the room with his eye contact.

I am an INFJ personality type according to the Myers-Briggs Type Indicator which is one of the most perceptive of all types. I tend to pick up on things very quickly. However, when I brought this situation up to my husband, he basically blew me off and advised me that I should become friends with her as she lacked female friendship, which was true. Let's just say that this was not his best advice. It's hard to become someone's friend when they are hitting on your husband. But nevertheless, I tried. Duh!

Over time, I felt unheard, minimized and I became extremely angry. I began to dread going to church where I had to face this situation every week. It wasn't just at church either, because she seemed to be everywhere. She was present at leadership meetings and all activities related to church. Suddenly church was no longer my "happy place." I continued to put on my pastor's wife smile and sat in the front row looking all together, but I was literally falling apart. No one really seemed to notice or care. Not even my husband who was sitting next to me on the front row. After all, the important thing was to focus on growing the church.

My husband is usually very attentive to my concerns. However, regarding this issue he would "gaslight" my concerns. "Gaslighting" is when someone intentionally makes someone doubt their memories or perception of reality. The term can be traced back to a 1938 play, British playwright Patrick Hamilton created, but most folks are most familiar with the 1944 adaptation with Charles Boyer and Ingrid Bergman. He would put my concerns back on me and my own insecurities.

Henry Cloud describes invalidation and "gaslighting" by the following:

"What is the number one thing that destroys connection and trust? Trust emerges when we can enter someone's reality, validate their experiences, and have ours validated by them as well. Connection and trust happen when one heart meets another. What destroys connection and trust like nothing else? Invalidation. Invalidation occurs when a person's experience is all that exists to him or her. And he or she then moves to negate the other person's experience, treating it as somehow not real or non-existent. You may also be familiar with the term "gaslighting" in this instance. Have you ever had this happen? It feels terrible. Especially when it comes from someone you care about or someone you need.

The sad thing is that most times the people who invalidate other people's experience are not aware that they are doing something destructive. In fact, they often think they are helping. We have all seen those instances where someone (maybe even ourselves) has said something negative like, "This is a really upsetting experience for me," and someone immediately comes back with, "C'mon, it wasn't that bad!" or some other attempt to help that only drives the person further into hopelessness, because now the person has two problems instead of one. They have the initial problem that they felt so negative about, and then they feel that they're all alone with no one who truly understands. That is why people who try to help others by talking them out of what they feel are usually no help at all. It is also the reason why research has for decades proven that you can help desperate people immensely by giving them no answers at all, and only giving them empathy. From childhood to corporate boardrooms, connection is key, and invalidation is a cancer."

So it was extremely painful to feel invalidated. This only drove me further into isolation. I am a woman so yes, I have insecurities. I had seen some infidelity issues in my own family of origin and had some real fears that this would someday happen to me. But these were normal fears, I do believe and through counseling have been reassured that these were not unreasonable concerns that I had.

My counselor assured me that if something is important to me, it should also be important to my spouse. I asked that he talk to someone about this woman and situation and be held accountable, which he did in a half-hearted sort of way. He admitted he sensed it as well and told me that he would be on guard against it. He intentionally withdrew from overt contact with her as much as possible when I was around but said that the more he focused on the withdrawal, the more power she seemed to have over him. This was something that came out during our healing process and counseling, after the fact. While he did not blame me for this issue, because of my anger and hostility toward him for his lack of attention to this matter, that merely made her adulation more appealing.

As my anger toward him increased so did her appeal. The anger, hurt, and betrayal that I was feeling began to become obsessive. The dynamics between us became quite tense. I remember one night waking up from a dream where I was hitting him as hard as I could. My cries for help went unnoticed. I also confided what I was going through to a friend in the congregation that I thought could be trusted. Not long after that, she and her husband left our congregation for various reasons. I had asked that we stay connected but when I tried to contact her there was no response. This was another big blow to my crushed spirit.

During this time there was one woman; Linda Kline, Pastoral Director of Psalm One Ministries (www. psalmone.org), a powerful ministry of Bible teaching and Christ-centered spiritual formation, as well as ministry to pastors and their families, who heard my voice. When I shared my situation at one of her pastor's wives soul care retreats, she recognized this immediately as transference. She had a master's in counseling psychology and master's in divinity from Trinity Evangelical Divinity School. She recommended the book, Sheep In Wolves' Clothing by Valerie McIntyre. Unfortunately, I put it off and failed to read the book until recently, but when I finally did after all of this took place, I saw clearly that it was truly classic transference. She was the only one who validated my concerns.

CHAPTER 7
THE CRASH

A S I REACHED MY MID-50S, the perfect storm seemed to be in place which resulted in a mental breakdown. My hurt and anger led to despondence, depression, and despair. During this time, I was going through menopause; a time of great change in a woman, both hormonally and emotionally. You can't help but feel that you are losing some of your female attractiveness, especially with all the media attention on the young and flawless female. You eventually reorient your life to greater values but during this time there is a great deal of uncertainty as to who you are as a woman. It is a time when a woman needs reassurance that she is still attractive and appealing to her husband and I wasn't receiving that. A great distance had developed between us. Here I had given my all to the church and this man, disrupting my life again and again only to find myself in this lonely and desolate place. I truly felt betrayed.

I was also in a season of loss as I seemed to be losing those I loved most in some way. My children left the nest and both of them eventually moved away. My parents who were divorced and lived over an hour each way, with me in the middle, required care in their later years and our roles had reversed. Eventually, there was the loss and grieving of their deaths and the handling of their estates, which fell on my shoulders as I was the only child in the area. My only brother lived out of state. These are huge transitions and losses to face in one's life.

My schedule was jam packed with activities. I was extremely busy and overwhelmed. There was no time to grieve or rest. I was working full time in a real estate office and continued to sell real estate. I was also mentoring college age girls one night a week, serving on the Pastoral Team, facilitating small groups, and attending an overwhelming number of church functions and additional activities. With the extreme busyness and over commitment, I felt absolutely exhausted physically and emotionally. I couldn't seem to get off this hamster wheel called life. My husband, who was so preoccupied with the church, was emotionally unavailable so that made me feel very much alone. His attention was obviously elsewhere and I sometimes felt that he didn't see me at all. Since my love language is "focused attention" to feel significant and valued are very important to me. The opposite is also true; to feel invisible or unnoticed is extremely painful for me and one that the church fed constantly.

In "Anatomy of the Soul," Curt Thompson states, "Being understood. Feeling felt. We value few experiences more, especially when we're in a distressing noxious emotional state." I felt my resentment build as I saw my husband engaging and giving out so much to others but not leaving much for us. During this time, when we found time to be alone or to get away together many times, he was so exhausted that he would honestly fall asleep in the most romantic of settings. I would not say that I am an overly "needy" sort of woman but I do enjoy the full attention of the man I am sharing my life with. I remember hearing Gail McDonald speak once regarding her marriage. She said that when talking about the church enters your bedroom, you are in trouble. I couldn't help thinking that we were there.

So I came to a point where I hit the wall and my life came to a crashing halt. I spiraled down into despair and depression and ended up spending several weeks in the Linder Center, which is a psychiatric hospital in Cincinnati. They stabilized me with medication and I went home. I did return to work and thankfully I was transferred to a slower office with the same company, because I was no longer able to keep up with all my duties. I found that I simply could not function at my normal pace. I tried getting back on the hamster wheel but it didn't seem to be working any longer. This "determined doer" and "just try harder" woman suddenly found herself in a place of utter exhaustion; spiritually, mentally, physically, and emotionally. A couple of times when I was with the particular woman that had caused me so much concern, my emotions were so fragile that I began to shake uncontrollably.

My doctor's solution, not knowing the underlying issues was to increase my medication and also add medication for anxiety. I became way over-medicated. Medication certainly has a purpose and can be quite helpful to stabilize the brain, but I became like a zombie and could not feel any emotion nor complete the simplest of tasks. I was extremely anxious and very disoriented. I didn't want to leave the house or be around people. I had been a competitive tennis player since my late 20's so it was unusual to find myself not being able to even follow through on hitting the tennis ball. I left the court one day and threw my racquet in my closet, thinking that was certainly being taken from me too. For about nine months, I did not attend church and eventually I had to give up my job entirely. It felt as though even God had left me and I felt totally alone. I basically laid on the couch in a fetal position and slept most of the day. It was not my favorite chapter. It was extremely hard for my family as well to watch me in this condition. After a really hard and difficult year or so for us all, I really got to where I really wanted to end it all.

CHAPTER 8

RESTORED

"I Have a New Attitude"

B UT GOD HAD OTHER PLANS and through an outpatient support group, He began to pick me up from the pit and restore my zest and vitality. Through prayer, support, and lots of love; I began to heal. I was able to get off of all the medication and thankfully, I have not needed any for more than six years. Recently a nurse practitioner came out to do a home assessment on me and since it had been over five years with no medication and no reoccurrence, she marked my condition as "Resolved." This raised my spirits tremendously.

Since my restoration, God has shown me through a variety of sources, some necessary changes I needed to make in order to live a healthier lifestyle. But all the credit goes to my Savior who lifted me up from the pit, brought the right people into my life, and restored my soul. I also credit my husband, family and friends for their faithfulness, support, prayers and love during this time.

Sometimes help came from the least expected sources such as a therapist, the doctor, or another patient. One therapist told me that she thought that my breakdown was actually a breakthrough. Her brother was a Catholic priest and had shared that sometimes this was true. I began to see God's presence everywhere. Love and healing came in particular, from an outpatient group and later follow up in a support group led by an outstanding Christian therapist. The group was for those with mental health issues and those in recovery from substance abuse. It was similar to an AA meeting and speaking from experience, I firmly believe in the power of these groups. This particular group included pilots, doctors, flight attendants, janitors, construction workers, homemakers and people from all walks of life. I had never been in such a powerful group. I had led and been in many small groups over the years in the church but this was different in a positive way. We were all walking together, supporting each other and sharing our struggles and our successes. I stay in contact with some of these people to this day.

I started embracing better self-care. I became intentional about removing myself from toxic people. I sought counseling for the past and coaching for my future and dealt with my need to not disappoint and please people. I started listening to my body and living within my God-given limits instead of pushing myself to exhaustion. As I began to heal so did my marriage and the gap between my husband and I began to close. George truly apologized and we worked through our issues with lots of communication with one another and the assistance of others. He said he would win my heart back and he did. We came out in a much better place. Honestly, I can look back on this chapter as a refining time for both of us and be thankful, though it's a chapter I hope to never repeat. We came out of it as different people, and we are both convinced of God's restorative power. I'll even add that I am back playing tennis again on the same level as I was previously. Another miracle, not a small one either, as it brings me much joy to be back at the sport I love.

During this season of depression and anxiety, I stayed away from church for about nine months. There was extreme concern shown by several women on behalf of my health, one of which was the woman I had particular concerns about. She called me every week and scheduled time for coffee. Little did I know that there were also a lot of calls also made to my husband to inquire as to how I was faring. This was a very vulnerable time for my husband, but thankfully I can say that he remained faithful to me in spite of great temptations. It convinced me of his intense love for me. During my illness, my husband did not know what the outcome would be. Our family doctor even advised George to leave me during this time as he was still a young man and didn't deserve to go through that kind of situation. Thankfully, he didn't heed that advice.

George thought he might have lost the love of his life for good. I believe he came to realize and appreciate the depth of love that he had for me. I also realized my love for him and appreciated his faithfulness to me during this time. Once my physical and mental health returned, he set up better boundaries in relating to the woman of my great concern and all women in general. I believe he came to see that my concerns were real and justified and not just in my head.

Once he set up better boundaries, there was an abrupt turn in this particular woman and several women's attitudes toward him. The English playwright and poet William Congreve Is known for these lines in his play, The Morning Bride, 1697: *Heav'n has no Rage, like Love to Hatred Turned, Nor Hell a Fury, like a Woman scorned.* There is much truth to this statement. There was increased anger and agitation towards my husband coming from these women. He and I both felt extreme tension when around them. They became increasingly disgruntled with things at church and with my husband's messages and leadership. There eventually came a point where they would come for the class prior to the service on Sunday and then leave the service before he spoke. A close friend who was entering the building one Sunday morning when this one particular woman and her husband were leaving was invited to go to breakfast with them, as she said that they weren't staying because George's sermons were lifeless and that he just basically read out of a book. This woman then requested that George release her from all her church duties. She said that she had lost her passion and wanted no further obligations at church. Their church attendance became sporadic during the last year of my husband's ministry. We heard rumors and accusations that got back to us from friends that these women were suggesting to others that George had abused his power and position, that he didn't promote women, that he was a controlling person and that his character was undermined in other ways as well. We were even invited by one couple in our congregation to come to their home for prayer as they felt we were under spiritual attack with these accusations. He was glad to get out of his pastoral role in this congregation.

In his defense, I felt that my husband had always tried to use his position wisely and for the greater good of the congregation. He has allowed, encouraged and provided for women to serve in their God-given capacity. There was also a very outspoken and demanding agenda coming from these women that he needed to ordain a woman elder or woman pastor in the congregation. While this was a good thing, he did not see the calling being manifested in anyone at that particular time. When he looked at me regarding this, I said, "Don't even think about it." Being a pastor or an elder is simply not my calling." While I do not diminish the title or office, I simply felt that my calling is to be a friend to others, especially women and not in a pastoral role.

I am thankful that by God's incredible grace, our marriage and situation ended well. I have had to look at some of my own issues and extend the grace and forgiveness of God. I have been healed of much of my anger but still battle triggers that can cause it to return. I have learned through this chapter many things I could not have learned otherwise. I had to let go of my own self-righteousness and as scripture states in I Corinthians 10:12 – "So if you think you are standing firm, be careful that you don't fall. We are all susceptible to temptation." I saw how I could be direct and demanding and sometimes lacked the grace that I so badly wanted and needed.

I am still very tenacious and determined but I am tenacious on the tennis court and for abiding in God and participating with Him as He directs my life. I came to realize my intense need for God. I have also come to see my self-worth in God's opinion of me, which is infinite love and came out in a much stronger position. In the future, should my husband decide that he no longer loves me, I'm sure it would be painful, but I will not fall apart. Because I married young, I honestly believe that his opinion was far too important to me. I jokingly told him recently that if he leaves me for someone else on Wednesday, I will grieve on Thursday and move on by Friday. He jested, "Only one day?" So I said, "Ok, maybe I will give you the weekend." I say this partly in jest, but I truly have a much stronger confidence/awareness of who I am. He was actually encouraged at this realization that I do not consider my worth and value to be dependent on him. That's a hard load for a man to bear. The bottom line is that my value and worth are not in what he or others think of me but in what God thinks of me. I am incredibly loved, significant and noticed by Him. I am learning to rest and live out of that love and deep center in my soul.

I also had to be reminded that the key to fighting our

battles is through prayer, fasting and surrender. God will truly fight our battles if we turn them over to Him. He will provide solutions and we can find rest. However, we still have our part to do and must participate as He shows the way. After my restoration and return to church, I would have triggers at church when I would see this particular woman week after week, it would begin to take me back to a negative place. I no longer wanted to feel all of the anger and hurt. I simply had no room for it in my heart. I found myself speaking abruptly and rudely to this woman. My husband was trying to figure out why I was having a hard time, when he reassured me that it was definitely over on his part. He couldn't quite understand why I just couldn't forget it and move on. But sometimes, it becomes necessary to remove ourselves from situations in order to allow our hearts to heal and to keep our wounds from reopening.

God has a sense of humor. I was able to use a situation that I believe God engineered to explain this to him. A friend of mine was in town so she, George and I went to a local restaurant for dinner. It was the first night on the job for our waiter whose name was Shane, so he was a bit nervous. I was trying to be very encouraging and when we left I told him that he did a great job and even mentioned to the manager that he did a good job. A couple of weeks later, we went to the same restaurant with our daughter and two grandkids for lunch. Shane spotted me and even though he wasn't our waiter, came running over to tell me hello. He said, "Hi Vicki, do you remember me?" I spotted his name tag and said, "Oh yes." He said, "I am so glad to see you again. How are you?" I replied that I was fine. He then said if I needed anything to let him know. As he left our table, my husband was fuming. My daughter was cracking up and said, "Mom, he was hitting on you." Well this continued a bit and George said several times, "I can't believe he was hitting on you with me sitting right here." I jokingly replied that maybe he thought you were my father, relishing the moment (Ok, maybe a bit too much). Forgive me, Lord!

As we were leaving, he came over smiled and said that he hoped I would return soon. My daughter said that she had never seen her dad so jealous. When we got in the car he was still visibly upset about how rude it was that this guy was showering me with attention right in front of him. It was then that I felt that it was the perfect moment to ask how it made him feel. He replied, "Very disrespected." So I explained to him that now he knew how I had felt every week at church. He suddenly "got it." It reminded me of the time in the biblical account when the prophet, Nathan got David's attention through a personal story that touched him emotionally.

The last year of George's pastoral role was incredibly difficult for him as he faced the wrath of these women. He was definitely ready to move on and out of that congregation. We have returned a couple of times for a visit and there are those that we continue to keep in touch with but we both decided that it was best for our marriage and both of our mental states to become part of a different church where we could start fresh and serve as equals in a new setting. Thankfully, God provided that church for us. I also really needed to get out of his shadow at church, which has happened at our new church.

My husband is a natural leader and he's especially good at casting a big shadow. While I truly admire his gifts and abilities, his personality is such that he always makes a large impact. I make an impact as well, but in a more subtle way. This didn't go over so well in our church setting where as the pastor, his voice always seemed to have the biggest impact. I had a hard time at church being myself. I could be myself in the business world, at home, on the tennis court, and with friends but somehow when we were at church he would end up being the center of attention and would out-shine me.

I met monthly with a spiritual director, who was an ordained Presbyterian pastor, and she told me over 20 years ago that she felt the Holy Spirit telling me that I needed to come out of his shadow, even then. It has taken awhile for new patterns to develop. He had to learn to step back and I had to learn to step forward. We had to learn a new dance. Since we are learning a new dance we sometimes step on each other's feet but we are learning how to work together in a healthier way . In our previous church, he was in an elevated role and we were not seen as equals. Now we are once again.

I share all of this with the hope that through our

story, male pastors will become more aware of the female transference issues within the body of Christ and what it can do to your wife's heart. This is my story and not everyone will be able to relate or understand because it's not their story. Many pastors have done a great job of excluding their wife from expectations of the congregation and remaining out of the emotional entanglements of female parishioners. We have learned many things over the years, both what to do and what not to do. In many ways, we did a lot of things very well, but certainly as we look back there are things we could have done better. My husband was a gifted pastor and served in this capacity in a worthy manner. He took that congregation and led them through many changes and left a strong and sturdy foundation. I certainly don't really fully understand the incredible pressures placed on him as a pastor. There are so many expectations and burdens to bear in that job.

There are many things that he has never shared with me simply because he felt my heart could not handle it. Many pastor's wives that I know are extremely happy and content but there are far too many who are not. There are many angry pastors' wives out there and I believe this could be partly due to the transference issue and all the female attention directed towards their husbands. The following sobering statistics gathered from HB London in 2016 reveal that 80% of pastors' wives feel left out and unappreciated by church members, 56% have no close friends in the church, 84% feel unqualified and discouraged in their roles, 80% feel pressured to do things and be something in the church that they are not, 80% feel their husband is over worked, 80% wish their husbands would choose another profession, 80% feel their husbands spend insufficient time with them, and 50% of pastor's marriages end in divorce. These statistics sadden me. Something is askew.

CHAPTER 9
BECOMING A PART OF THE SOLUTION
ADVICE FOR THE OTHER WOMEN

I F YOU ARE A WOMAN and are feeling infatuated with your pastor, please consider the following: he may be gifted, love the Lord and have a heart to serve, but he is a man with flaws of his own that you may not see clearly. Also remember that beside him is his spouse who has sacrificed and given far more than anyone sees for his career. There is someone who has had her life and family disrupted on many occasions. There is someone who has scheduled her life around the church calendar and who has picked her husband off the floor, literally or emotionally on resignation Monday, when he is totally spent from a weekend of ministry and ready to call it quits. Beside him is someone who may be trying to meet the demands of her own career and the home so her husband can be available to others in their time of need. The spouse of a pastor is someone who does not have a pastor and could probably use a little bit more emotionally from her husband. Before you call the pastor just to talk about what's going on in your life and family, realize that you are taking some of his emotional energy away from her.

My advice is to develop more female friendships to share

your life and inner most secrets with. Please don't discuss your personal issues with your pastor. Go to a professional or another woman. I have noticed that most women who lack female friends have been the ones who have felt the most need to counsel with my husband. Furthermore, if by chance, a pastor's wife does share a frustration she is having with her husband with a group of women, please do not come to the pastor's defense and dismiss her concerns. Realize that while a pastor's wife may have her smile on and appear very well put together on Sundays and at other times, this doesn't mean that she isn't totally exhausted and hurting inside from juggling so many balls in the air. Be kind to your sister and do not wound her heart merely so you can get your emotional needs met by her husband. Getting entangled with a married man is the worst wound you can inflict on another woman. Set good boundaries in this area and be respectful to both your pastor and his wife. One good boundary would be to never text, call or email your pastor without copying in your spouse or including them on the call.

Consider also what you are doing to your own husband and his heart as he sees you gushing all over the pastor. Consider his feelings as he sees this playing out right in front of his eyes week after week. Save your affections for your husband and maybe instead of making the pastor's favorite dish, why not make your husband's favorite dish instead. Shower him with your affection instead of the pastor. The marriage bond is sacred and for anyone to mess with that is treading on dangerous ground, male or female. You will not come out unscathed.

CHAPTER 10
ADVICE TO PASTORS

ONE SUGGESTION TO AVOID a Pastor Disaster is to read the Book of Proverbs. There are many warnings to men regarding the dangers of a seductive woman. A thorough study of this area would be helpful to do in a group or on your own. Transference that can lead to an emotional or literal affair is nothing to play around with. You will pay the utmost price. I believe that God places the man, especially as a pastor, as the responsible party to truly guard his heart continually.

The following scriptures convey much:

Proverbs 5:1 – my son pay attention to my wisdom, listen well to my words of insight that you may maintain discretion and your lips may preserve knowledge. For the lips of an adulterous drip honey and her speech is smoother than oil. But in the end she is bitter as gall, sharp as a double-edged sword. Her feet go down to death, her steps lead straight to the grave. She gives no thought to the way of life, her paths are crooked but she knows it not.

5:8 – Keep to a path far from her, do not go hear the door of her house lest you give your best strength to others and your years to one who is cruel.

5:11 – At the end of your life you will groan when your flesh and body are spent. You will say, how I hated discipline, how my heart spurned correction! I would not obey my teachers or listen to my instructors.

5:14 – I have come to the brink of utter ruin in the midst of the whole assembly

Proverbs 6:24 – keeping you from the immoral woman, from the smooth tongue of the wayward wife...

6:25 – Do not lust in your heart for her beauty or let her captivate you with her eyes.

6:26 – For the adulteress preys upon your very life

6:27 – Can a man scoop fire into his lap without his clothes being burned. Can a man walk on hot coals without his feet being scorched. So is he who sleeps with another man's wife, no one who touches her will go unpunished.

6:32 – a man who commits adultery lacks judgment, whoever does so destroys himself. Blows and disgrace are his lot, and his shame will never be wiped away.

Proverbs 7:5 – They will keep you from the adulteress, from the wayward wife with her seductive words

7:21 – She seduced him with her smooth talk

7:22 – All at once he followed her like an ox going to the slaughter, like a deer stepping into the noose till an arrow pierces his liver, like a bird darting into a snare little knowing it will cost him his life.

Proverbs 9:17,18 – Stolen water is sweet. Food eaten in secret is delicious but little do they know that the dead are there, that her guests are in the depths of the grave.

Proverbs 22:14 – The mouth of an adulteress is a deep pit, he who is under the Lord's wrath will fall into it.

22:26 – My son give me your heart and let your eyes keep to my ways, for a prostitute is a deep pit and a wayward wife is a narrow well. Like a bandit she lies in wait and multiplies the unfaithful among men.

Proverbs 30:20 – This is the way of an adulteress, she eats and wipes her mouth and says, I have done nothing wrong. My absolute favorite: Post it in a prominent place.

Proverbs 5:15 – Drink water from your own cistern, running water from your own well. May your fountains be blessed and may you rejoice in the wife of your youth. A loving doe, a graceful deer, may her breasts satisfy you always, may you ever be captivated by her love. Why be captivated my son by an adulteress. Why embrace the bosom of another man's wife? For a man's ways are in full view of the Lord and he examines all his paths.

Flattery and smooth talk are common traps for men throughout these passages. Don't be seduced by the flattery of other women. Listen to the concerns of your wife. She is most likely your greatest fan.

CHAPTER 11
LOVE YOUR LADY

FIRST OF ALL, ONE OF THE MOST important things you can do for your special lady out there is to let the congregation know how much she means to you. A pastor once told George to tell the congregation often that you love them. While this might be a good thing, my advice is to tell them often how much you love your wife. We used to return from vacation and my heart would ache when he would tell everyone how much he missed them. I wanted him to tell them the truth. That we had a great time, with great sex and lots of great talks and that he didn't miss them one bit.

Proverbs 30:21 – Under three things the earth trembles, under four it cannot bear up...an unloved woman who is married. In most cases, a woman will gladly give up attention from her husband for an immediate, urgent need. But when this becomes a pattern over many years, a woman can start to feel very resentful. Pastor can also be synonymous with overseer or elder.

Titus 1:6 – An elder must be blameless, **faithful to his wife**, a man whose children believe and are not open to be the charge of being wild and disobedient.

I Tim 3:2 – The overseer is to be above reproach, **faithful to his wife**, temperate, self-controlled, respectable, hospitable, able to teach. When the office of pastor or elder is mentioned in the New Covenant, there is always the admonition of being faithful to one's wife. This is a huge requirement for this calling, position and title.

The Book of Proverbs says that it is better to dwell on the rooftop than in the house with an angry woman. I think we can all agree, if mama ain't happy, ain't nobody happy. I'm talking in general terms here, realizing that there are extremely dysfunctional circumstances. A pastor's influence is greatly enhanced when he is in a happy marriage. If you find yourself in tempting circumstances and lacking the love you once had for your wife, maybe it's time for counseling or a sabbatical to restore a broken relationship. It may save your life. If you find yourself being seduced by a flattering woman, be like the patriarch Joseph who ran out of the house and left his cloak when seduced by Potiphar's wife. Don't linger.

Give yourself completely to Jesus but not to the church. There will always be more needs to fill than you can possibly meet. When Jesus left this earth, there were still people who needed to be healed, and still demons to be cast out. But he was confident that He had finished what the Father sent him to do. That's all that is required; to do what God, not the church asks of you. Don't burn yourself out. Get away often with God, your spouse, and family. Have a trusted spiritual companion that allows you to safely share your deepest heart. Realize that this is a position and title for a time and be prepared to give it up when that time comes to an end. Being a pastor is not your identity and it is not forever, it will come to an end.

CHAPTER 12
SPOUSES OF PASTORS

———————

T O MY SISTERS WITH SPOUSES in full time ministry, realize that in general women are gifted with an insight that men do not possess. I believe that is one reason why we can be a helpmate from a position of strength in lots of areas. When we sense or have concerns about a particular situation, or a particular woman in the congregation, we should bring it to our husband's attention. Now, we must also remember that we have our own brokenness and wounds which can cause us to be wrong as well. There is always that possibility, but if something is important to us, it should also be important to our spouse. Bring it out into the open and if necessary pursue further counseling or help from other sources. Do not let your voice be invalidated or minimized. You are not crazy and it's not all in your head. Even if it comes out that you are insecure in certain areas, that is something your spouse should be aware of and sensitive to as well. But many times, we as women may see something long before our husband does. Do not dismiss your concerns and do not let your husband dismiss them either. Over the years, my husband has learned to value and appreciate my intuition. I have also learned to appreciate his strength in areas where I am vulnerable. Please remember to seek God first so He can show you how to deal with sensitive situations.

In several church meetings, I was a bit annoyed that I was constantly encouraged to keep making the pastor happy. Well, that's all fine and good but what about your needs? God wants you to feel loved, to be noticed, and to be cherished. It's not always all about their needs. It's important to express to your husband how he can meet your needs. It's a mutual relationship of giving and receiving. It's not all about one person getting their needs met only, but both should feel their needs are being fulfilled.

Our regional pastor's wife and several other pastors' wives and I were together at an informal gathering. The regional pastor was truly quite gifted in relationship skills and working with people but he lacked organizational skills and was "structurally challenged." The wife had great skills in that area and worked tirelessly behind the scenes to cover for him in that area. Everyone marveled at how much he could accomplish, but we all knew the main reason was because of her. She told us that she sometimes felt like a "Wonderbra," because she made it look like there was more there than it really was. Well, we had a good laugh from that because I had never heard it expressed quite like that.

Refuse to walk in anyone's shadow. Live out of your own God-given passions. If you are a people pleaser as I was, know that you simply can't please everyone and coming to that realization is very liberating. You are not an extension of your husband. You are a unique masterpiece. You are like no other being ever created since the beginning of time, you are incomparable, you are a one of a kind expression of the image of God. The comparison trap will steal your joy. Oscar Wilde, an Irish Poet and Playwright said it best, "Be yourself, because everyone else is already taken."

CHAPTER 13
WALKING IN VICTORY

S OMEWHERE ALONG THE ROAD OF LIFE, I realize that I had lost myself. I had been so busy making others happy and getting pulled into their pool that I forgot who I was. God told me that my pool is magnificent and that I needed to stay in that area. Colossians 3:3 states, *"For you died, and your life is now hidden with Christ in God."* A similar passage in Colossians 2:3- says, *"In whom are hidden all the treasures of wisdom and knowledge."* So I deepened my quest to get to know this being who knows me intricately, who formed me in my mother's womb. Therefore, as I got to know Him more deeply I truly found myself. I believe this is one of the mysteries of knowing Christ, that by knowing Him more we come to more fully know ourselves. When we know ourselves, we can be free to remove the fig leaves (it all started with Adam and Eve in the Garden), the things we hide behind, the false self. If you try to let the world define you, you will never be enough. You will always be inadequate. To be fully known and fully loved, is everyone's desire. That begins with the realization that this is true of us in Christ. That is part of the freedom of knowing Christ, as John 8:36- says, *"And when the Son has set you free, you are free indeed."*

Now you might be thinking this girl has some real issues. My pastor's wife doesn't feel any of this. Don't be so sure. Whenever I get in a safe place with pastor's wives, this issue usually comes up. When I speak about my book, almost invariably a pastor's wife will ask if they can write a chapter. So, this book could have been much longer. I may plan to do a sequel where other pastor's wives may share their stories. Many have been more bizarre than mine. I have heard stories of stalking and eventually needing to get a restraining order to prevent women from calling and coming to a pastor's home. There have been stories of women peeking in windows to watch the pastor.

One friend of mine who is also the spouse of a pastor, had concerns about a particular woman for years and hit the ceiling when this woman called and asked for the pastor to come and anoint her at home while she was sick in bed. He was planning to go when my friend prayed and the lady became so contagious that he couldn't go. Praise God! Do I need to add that this is not a good idea? Yikes! You can't make some of this stuff up.

I heard a pastor's wife speak at a conference several years ago. She shared that her husband was the pastor of a huge fast-growing church. A woman in the congregation set her sights on him and there was an emotional entanglement. While he responded only through emails, the church took action and dismissed the pastor. They then left the state to rebuild their lives which was extremely traumatic. But the story continues when the woman continued to contact the pastor and when he responded once more, the new church took the same action. Devastated, they had to rebuild and their lives were ripped apart, again. Perhaps more awareness and accountability would resolve some of these issues. This stuff is real.

Although, this was a painful chapter to share, it was merely a chapter. Thankfully, most of our ministry years were positive. Now in this season of our lives, we hope to help minister to other couples on their journey in full time ministry, which is unlike any other profession. The last emotion I am looking for is sympathy, empathy perhaps, but not sympathy. A few years ago, I was blessed to reunite with two college friends in Hawaii. I found myself in the refreshing and beautiful waters of the Pacific Ocean. I felt the Holy Spirit impress upon my spirit that He was healing and washing away very painful memories. So, as the waves rolled over me I felt renewed and healed. What a perfect setting for a healing.

It has also been seven years since this dark night of my soul. The number seven has great significance in the Bible as the number of completeness and perfection (both physical and spiritual). I am ready to move forward. I do not believe I could have written this book and talked about these things openly, had I not received complete healing in some of these areas. I'm not saying that I don't need more healing and wholeness in other areas and I welcome that in my future. Life is actually a process of moving toward wholeness and maturity.

I found out through this trial how frail I am when I try to handle things out of my own strength and I proclaim, Never again! I also understand how resilient and strong I am when I cooperate with God, his guidance and power, as well as the incredible support all around me. The lyrics from the song, "Just Be Held," convey that instead of holding on, sometimes, you just need to let go and just be held. Your world's not falling apart, it's falling into place. In the end, it's probably not the holding on that will summarize our lives. It is the letting go that will be of the greatest significance. Letting go is not an easy process, especially if we've earned our reputation as being tenacious, stubborn and having the ability to preserve against tremendous odds. These may be good traits to get us through at times, but the truth is, at some point we also need to have the strength to let go and receive help. At a Marriage Retreat recently, we did a "trust fall" off of a platform into the arms and hands of our small group. It was scary and yet incredible, to release control and fall backwards knowing that you would be caught.

I faced some of my greatest fears and for a time felt totally out of control and yet retained my sanity in the end (some might argue that point). I came through this trial with a sound mind and body and less fearful and more filled with the love of Christ than ever before. This trial produced a deeper connection to Christ and to others. It's amazing how God can take our worst situation and bring good out of it. That's what Paul says, in Romans 8:28, that

ALL things work together for good for those who love God and walk according to His purpose. I experienced the love and care of the shepherd that left the 99 and went after that one lost sheep, which was me. I also felt that same "Good Shepherd" fulfillment of Psalms 23 in my life. That Psalm is now personal. He restored my soul, he led me to still waters, He anointed my head with oil and he prepared a table in the midst of my enemies. When I felt so alone He showed up and whispered his words of love and courage in my ear. He paid the ultimate cost for me because He's just that good. This is what is known as the paschal mystery. Out of death, comes life. From the cross, comes new life and resurrection. From the resurrection comes the ascension. We are raised with Christ to heavenly places.

George Matheson (1842-1906), known as the Blind Scottish Preacher, struggled with his eyesight all of his life. He had hoped to marry a young woman but she refused because he was mostly blind. He became a very famous preacher and people would travel from great distances to hear him. He packed the churches when he spoke. In 1885 he was invited to come and preach to Queen Victoria and the queen was so moved by the sermon that she asked for it to be printed out and published for more people to be able to receive it. But perhaps one of his greatest pieces that Matheson ever wrote was a simple hymn, which he wrote on the night his sister was wed. Overall, he was a very joyful person, but perhaps the memory of the young woman who refused to wed him because of his blindness brought him to a place of great anguish and pain. He penned this hymn in about 5 minutes on a napkin which is entitled "O Love that Will Not Let Me Go." That hymn came as the result of a time of his most severe mental suffering. He said he felt it dictated to him by some inward voice. I discovered this hymn after I came through my own time of intense pain. I played the version of this hymn by Indelible Grace many times a day. I still refer to it often as the words have ministered to me over and over and they still bring a tear. The lyrics are as follows:

O Love that wilt not let me go,
I rest my weary soul in Thee;
I give Thee back the life I owe,
That in Thine ocean depths its flow
May richer, fuller be.
O Light that follows all my way,
I yield my flickering torch to Thee;
My heart restores its borrowed ray,
That in Thy sunshine's blaze its day
May brighter, fairer be.
O Joy that sleekest me through pain,
I cannot close my heart to Thee;
I trace the rainbow through the rain,
And feel the promise is not vain,
That morn shall tearless be.
O Cross that liftest up my head,
I dare not ask to fly from Thee;

I lay in dust life's glory dead.
And from the ground there blossoms red
Life that shall endless be.

Give God your mess and let Him make a miracle. My favorite quote from Corrie Ten Boom is "No pit is so deep that He is not deeper still; with Jesus even in our darkest moments, the best remains and the very best is yet to be."

I do also know from experience that toxic emotions, if not dealt with can contribute to sickness in our bodies and minds. So much is coming to light in the area of neuroscience and the effects of negative thoughts on our body, as well as the opposite, that life giving thoughts can actually create more neuro pathways resulting in new dendrites and connections, causing our brains to begin flourishing. "Forgiveness truly frees us," says Dr. Carolyn Leaf, a Christian neuroscientist that has some incredible books and videos on detoxifying our brains so we can thrive. This only confirms what God told us a long time ago in Romans 12:2 about renewing our minds. There is tremendous power in our thoughts.

As I reclaimed myself, I began to notice the extraordinariness of the ordinary. God restored my vibrancy, appreciation, and zest for life. At the beginning of each year I ask God for a word. Two years ago, it was "resilient," a year ago it was "vibrant," and as this coming year approaches, I am hearing, "courageous." It has taken that to get this story out to all of you.

A couple of years ago one of the ladies in a share group I was participating in went to the Linder Center. I shared with my support group at St. Elizabeth, that I really wanted to go visit her but really was fearful to return. This was not exactly a "happy place" for me. After our support session, one of the participants asked if I would stay after. He then spoke to me advising that I really should consider returning to the Linder Center and that he felt I would feel a whole new sense of freedom by doing so. He also told me that once I realized that this period of my life was actually a gift that would be used to help others, then I would be further down the road to healing. Because I respected his opinion and advice I decided to return. I drove up to the facility. I felt anxious going through the locked doors but I kept going to visit my friend. She was extremely appreciative that I would do this for her. Some of the staff remembered me and expressed joy that I was doing so well. When I left, it was a clear sunny day and I looked up into the sky and felt intense gratitude. I was truly free! This reminded me of a scene in the movie, "Shaw Shank Redemption," (my husband's favorite movie) where the character; Andy Dufresne emerges from the muck and mire and comes out lifting his arms to heaven as a free man. I celebrated that I was not where I once was. I was walking in freedom.

If you have failed, do not despair or fear. Let it be a springboard to change and greater growth. We can claim the victory we all have in Christ and experience His abundant life. As I come to the conclusion of this part of my story, I would like to conclude with Psalms 66, it's like a sandwich where the Psalmist starts out by praising God and remembering his great works in the past, and it ends by trusting Him for answered prayer in the future. However, the substance between isn't very pleasant. Verses 10-12 seem a little contradictory, "For you, O God, tested us; you refined us like silver. You brought us into prison and laid burdens on our backs. You let men ride over our heads, we went through fire and water but you brought us to a place of abundance." Does this sound like a loving God? Well if a place of abundance was the end result of these hardships, then the answer is yes. A relationship with God is full of twists and turns and many obstacles. He gives us every reason to question Him and His goodness and faithfulness. But if we will continue to abide in Him and trust the process we will see His goodness shine through. He will stretch our faith through our trials.

A few years ago, we went to the beach with my husband's family. It was a small three-bedroom cottage and there were about 20 of us staying together for one week. Since I need my alone time, I would go out with a cup of tea and my journal early in the morning to see the sun rise and have a time of prayer. I found a nice bench tucked away in the tall grass. I had a perfect view of the ocean and it was quite nice. On the third day, I lathered up with my coconut oil and headed out to my spot. I did notice that the breeze had stopped and the wind was not blowing that particular day. So as I sat down, some disturbing little sand gnats began to appear. Their number increased greatly until I was unable to sit quietly. So, I jumped up and had to get out of there. Looking ahead, I saw the fishing pier and decided to go up there. It was quiet except for a few fishermen. I went to the end and found a comfortable bench. This was even more perfect than the previous spot. As I turned my head to the right there was the most spectacular rainbow in the sky. Rainbows have always been a special sign of God's faithfulness and hope. I realized that because of those gnats I had reached a better destination. I had been very comfortable in my original spot and would have stayed there had those gnats not drove me crazy and caused me to move on. I came out in a better place and no longer wished to return to my original spot. Remember weeping may linger for the night, but joy comes with the morning. (Psalms 30:5). As that hymn by George Matheson reminds us, "Trace the rainbow through the rain."

A good example of healthy boundaries and one who finished strong in the area of faithfulness to one's mate was Billy Graham. He was often away from home and yet always made sure he was accountable and did not meet with women alone. There would have been countless opportunities for failure on his part but it never happened due to his intentionality and accountability. Thankfully there was never any impropriety on his part in that area. I think we are quick to jump on the bandwagon and blame the pastor, when an affair does occur and yes, he should be the one most accountable, but why wait until there is a problem. I propose putting safeguards in place and giving men a safe place to share their weaknesses, difficulties in their marriage and ministry attractions openly. Sin loses its power when it comes into the light. When getting together, pastors need more awareness and accountability on matters of the heart instead of always talking about the latest church growth plan. They need more focus on spiritual renewal and church transformation, instead of increasing the size of their church with the latest church growth strategy. This would result in healthier churches which would then become a beacon of light to a confused and dazed world.

Strong marriages leave behind a lasting legacy for our children, grandchildren, churches, and the world. A strong husband/wife team is a huge blessing that can change and transform the world. It is not my desire to diminish your zeal and desire to serve God and advance His Kingdom. On the contrary, my hope is to inspire you to press forward, avoid pitfalls and distractions, and finish well.

And lastly and most importantly, I want to thank and applaud my husband for his vulnerability and support in addressing this issue. We met at college and I thought I had all my ducks in a row about getting my MBA and working as a Human Resource Manager. I figured I may marry and have children one day in my far away future. But as we got to know each other and I looked into those gorgeous brown eyes, fell in love, all my ducks got out of line. But who really cares about those freaking ducks anyway. We said, "I do" over 42 years ago and he still makes my heart skip a beat. He has lent his full support to this book from day one. He encouraged me to keep writing when I wanted to throw in the towel and give up this project. We have reached a new intimacy and love for each other that grows daily. We have made a good team and I am thankful we have shared life together thus far.

Thank you for traveling this chapter with me. Every day is a new page in your story. Don't be allured by the apparent "greener" grass on the other side. Be faithful to God and one another. I wish you every joyful blessing both now and in the world to come.

George Speaks

CHAPTER 14
MY #METOO

I CATEGORICALLY ACKNOWLEDGE that people receive unwanted, and unsolicited sexual advances and contact from others. In fact I've had my own #MeToo experience.

Sometime ago I was boarding a plane in Cincinnati for a flight to India. As I was standing in line to have my boarding pass checked a woman, probably twenty years younger than me came up beside me in line and stood next to me. I motioned her to go ahead of me, which I thought was the courteous thing to do. I assumed she was anxious to get on board and settled for the long flight ahead. I was not so anxious knowing I was going to be stuck in that seat for the next twelve hours.

After being cleared I headed down the gangway to the plane. I noticed her standing to the side on her phone. I assumed she was sending a last minute text. I walked by her with no eye contact, or verbal acknowledgment. When I was just a few steps from stepping on the plane someone grabbed a handful of my butt and squeezed. I'm sure I jumped a couple of feet off the ground and let out a loud, "Whoa!" I turned around and there she was. She said, "Sorry, I just can't help myself, I love salt and pepper."

I'm sure she was referring to my hair and beard, which is mostly "salt" with very little "pepper."

Now, I let her go in front of me again, and let a couple of other people go ahead as well, to distance myself from her, because I didn't want to experience some other unwanted contact and I didn't have any intention of joining the Mile High Club. As we boarded the plane I was thankful that she was directed to the opposite aisle from me, and I thought the encounter was over. I got seated and was getting settled in for the long flight ahead.

There was some mix up between my traveling companion whose assigned seat was beside me, and another gentleman. As they were trying to sort it out I heard a female voice standing beside me say, "I'll sit there." I looked up and there was the same lady pointing to seat beside me. My response was, "No, they will get it worked out."

I was a bit stunned by the whole situation, and thought, maybe I should tell someone. But I thought if I do, I probably wouldn't be believed or I'd be told I should feel flattered. The few times I've shared the experience that is exactly the response I've gotten; you should feel flattered. Honestly, it left me feeling a little bit vulnerable. In a very small way, and I don't mean to suggest that my experience is in any way comparable to what women experience, but it did give me a glimpse into what it must be like to experience unwanted and unsolicited sexual aggression.

The only reason I tell my #Me Too story is to say I know people, and no doubt women or children in the majority, and sometimes even men, experience unwanted, unsolicited and uninvited and inappropriate sexual aggression. And I know in a very small way how vulnerable and helpless it can leave you feeling. I can't tell you how many times I've thought about my experience and tried to project myself in the role of a woman, and how defenseless it must leave them feeling. The whole experience has made me a lot more empathetic towards the #Me Too movement. Again, the reason I share my story, is not in any way to suggest I understand what women go through, but only to say I know it occurs.

MINISTERS SIN TOO

I REMEMBER VIVIDLY MY ORDINATION to ministry in the fall of 1984. I was honored, humbled and nervous all at the same time. I remember it well but there is one thing that stands out to me more than anything else to this day. Immediately after the ceremony and even before we left the platform, where the ceremony took place, one of the pastors who participated in the ordination placed his hand on my shoulder and said, "The first thing you will learn as a minister is that ministers sin too."

Wow, did he know me better that I thought, was this a warning, a caution, a confession, or just a statement of reality. As it turns out, it was at least a statement of reality, because I'm certain that my first act as an ordained minister was, to sin. Yes, ministers sin too and ordination does not immunize you against it. If anything, the urge to sin may become more powerful, because of the attacks of Satan and his desire to bring you down, in some churches it is the need to appear perfect and have it all together, or the isolation which often occurs in ministry. All of these eat at your soul, because you know you don't have it all together and to live as if you do is to maintain a lie, which is a sin.

So let me be very clear, ministers sin too, and by all

means avoid those who might suggest otherwise. I had an associate pastor once that I had difficulty getting a straight answer out of, even in the most innocuous of situations. When we spoke about it and I told him I was having difficulty with the truthfulness of some of the things he told me. He was quite insulted and told me in no uncertain terms that he had not lied in over twenty years. I was so dumbfounded and didn't know how to respond, because even if I didn't think I had lied in twenty years, I certainly would have never said that. If I had of said it, it would have been a lie. A week later I asked him to clarify what he meant because I was struggling to get my head around it. After much conversation it came down to; as long as what he said to me was true, even if I was deceived and his intent was to deceive me, he was not lying. Needless to say, there was very little trust between us and the relationship went downhill.

Aren't ministers better than that? Well, the reality check is that ministers are human too. They deal with their personal weaknesses, struggles and wounds just like everyone else, and ordination doesn't heal or wash them away. I've heard respectable theologians say that the Bible can be a dangerous book in the hands of the unconverted. I'm certain we have all been witness to this. I'll add to that, that the ministry can be a dangerous profession in the hands of the flawed, and we are all flawed. This is just a reality check.

If a minister's top priority is not their own personal

devotional life and spiritual growth it can eventually lead to shipwreck. Unfortunately, doing ministry can end up being a veiled substitute for personal spiritual growth. After all, you are committed to and busy doing things for God. Even sermon preparation which involves Bible study and prayer can become about how to explain and illustrate a text in order to impact others, without thought to how it impacts me personally.

I know of pastors who have had severe moral failures, abused their position of spiritual authority, and deeply wounded totally innocent people. But I don't know or know of any pastor who entered the ministry with the intent of using their position in a predatory way. I'm not naïve enough to believe this has never occurred but I don't personally know anyone who has done this. The cases I'm aware of are people who have entered the ministry with a genuine desire to serve God, live an exemplary life, and advance his kingdom. Of course Satan has other ideas; seeking to steal, kill and destroy. There are many people who have had their lives destroyed by the moral failings of a minister.

The ministry is a unique job. As a minister you seek to be empathetic, available, a good listener, and present to people when they are in the most painful and joyous emotional times of their lives. Ironically, the better you are at doing your job, the more susceptible you become to transference.

MY WEAKNESSES

ONE OF MY GREATEST WEAKNESSES and challenges has been my self-sufficiency. Initially we may think that is a virtue and desired attribute, but even good things can become idols and our strengths can become our weaknesses. It started in my early childhood with the death of my father when I was four years of age. I have journeyed through life without a father figure and no one that I could look to as my provider, comforter, or counselor. Life taught me at a very early age that if I wanted something done, I would have to do it, and if I wanted something I would have to get it for myself.

My self-sufficiency served me quite well for several decades. I started doing farm work at eight years of age and working in a family run department store at ten. Being really good at saving money I bought a new car at sixteen and payed my way through college with no help from anyone. It served me well in the corporate world and later in ministry when I made a career change.

As I approached the age of fifty it all came crashing down. My self-sufficiency had become an idol and messiah, and a block between God and me. In dramatic fashion and a move of his grace I crashed only to discover that My

Heavenly Father had been with me all along. My greatest strength had become my greatest weakness and through my weakness my Father is now revealing himself.

Another weakness, again originating from my childhood, was finding validation outside of my family. I was very susceptible to praise and flattery, especially from women. There is much about the origin of this that I won't share for the sake of my family, but it was real and played heavily into what transpired and wounded Vicki to the core. As I reflect on these two things, I believe they played a huge role in what transpired. Although a physical affair never happened and I seriously doubt it would have ever happened, an emotional interplay did occur which deeply wounded Vicki, and for which I deeply regret.

So Who is to Blame?

———————————

I T SEEMS TO ME THAT WE ARE LIVING in an environment today that wants to quickly assign blame. There are certainly situations that are very clear and the assignment of blame appropriate and necessary. There are also situations that are not so clear cut and the blame is shared. It is not my place here to elaborate on those but only to say they do exist. The problem, as I see it is, once blame has been assigned it's easy to believe the problem has been dealt with and solved, and I don't think that is the case. It also seems to me that the purpose of assigning blame is to shame someone, which does not address the issue at its core. Perhaps the least productive thing to do is assign blame and walk away, thinking something has actually been accomplished.

I believe a better question to ask is, "Who bears responsibility?" In my case, I believe there are several parties that share responsibility. First, I accept full responsibility for the part that I played, which contributed to the situation Vicki describes. When she first came to me with her concerns, rather than listening to her and validating her concerns, I was dismissive and responded with, "It's all in your head." I knew she was right but quickly gas lighted, deflecting it all back to her.

Second, I'd have to say my ministry training shares some responsibility. In 33 years of pastoral ministry not once did the subject or anything related to transference come up. In my seminary training there was never any education on the issue. It's my understanding that part of professional counseling training includes training in the potential of transference and setting proper boundaries with a client. In thirty-three years of seminary and pastoral training there was not one mention of the potential for transference.

Third is ministry itself. Before making a career change to full time ministry I had a successful position with an aerospace corporation writing proposals and negotiating contracts. I know the stress of the corporate world but it does not compare to the stress of pastoral ministry. No doubt we have all heard the staggering numbers of those going into ministry that don't stay long enough to retire from ministry. I always knew it was stressful on my family but didn't realize just how stressful until I retired. Someone asked me if I missed pastoral ministry. My response, "Yes, it's like having a 700 pound gorilla lifted from your shoulders." If I had the choice to make today, I'd make the same choice, but I'd be much better prepared for what was ahead.

It has been said that pastoral ministry is the loneliest of professions. Many pastors feel isolated and have no place to share their burdens and struggles in a safe and non-judgmental environment. Even the pastor gatherings and associations I've been a part of have not provided that environment. Even there you must maintain the false façade of perfection and having it all together.

Too often pastors are faced with high expectations and low support, which can only lead to problems. Three is something terribly wrong and destructive in how we are doing church. I don't believe this is what Christ intended. Fourth are the women involved, who had some responsibility. I'm not trying to cast the blame on them but they do share some responsibility. If you think that women are not drawn to a pastor who is kind, caring, and empathetic and in a position of spiritual authority, then you are incredibility naïve. They have their own personal and marital issues that play a role.

And fifth of course is Satan; who desires to take us down and destroy everyone and the church and he will certainly use our weaknesses against us to do so.

The bottom line is that transference is real and it is going to occur. It's not a matter of if it will occur but when will it occur. It will have its subtle beginning in the most innocent situation and genuine ministerial efforts between flawed human beings. When it does will you have the awareness and humility to acknowledge it and will you be equipped to deal with in in a loving and graceful way. I was not, and willingly accept the bulk of the responsibility, or if you wish, the blame.

To Vicki, the person in my life who I love, cherish and respect above all others, I say, "It was not all in your head."

A FINAL WORD FROM VICKI

AS THE BOOK COMES TO AN END

I'll give you a second as you let my husband's words sink in. Of course, I cannot leave it there. As you can see, it was a difficult road for the two of us. It is easy to say that our lives have moved on, and they have, but at what cost? Pain, wounds, and loneliness: I can talk about it now without sinking into depression or replaying the visuals over and over in my head. This book was conceived in pain and birthed in a renewed mind and spirit. It is my prayer that this book will help you, especially if this has been your experience as a pastor's wife or a wife of a man who missed the reality that a particular woman was assigned to destroy a marriage. So, as we enter a new season, our bond is stronger than ever. We've finished that chapter and are entering a new season in our marriage and our ministry.

Today, we feel that part of our current ministry is similar to Aaron and Hur, who brought Moses a stone to sit on and held up his hands when he grew fatigued and weary. As long as they held up his arms, the Israelites continued to win the battle. Ministry can be lonely, and one can grow weary. We want to walk alongside ministry leaders to hold up their hands and strengthen them and their marriages as much as possible so that the battle is won. There are many obstacles and setbacks along the way, but the beauty of our Christian journey is that we learn and grow, from which we can then can help others grow and navigate their journeys. Lastly, please remember, "it's not all in your head," ladies. In general, God has equipped women with special discernment when it comes to relationship matters. Own it and listen to that spirit of discernment. God placed it there on the inside of you for a reason. Do not mismanage it. Use wisdom. If you lack wisdom, ask God for his word says, "If any of you lacks wisdom, you should ask God, who gives generously to all without finding fault, and it will be given to you." *James 1:5 NIV*.

Men, do not immediately think your wife is jealous of another woman. Tap into the wisdom of God and lean into the truth that comes from your wife. Hear her concerns when she comes to you. Take a step back and pray to ask God to allow you to see supernaturally. When He shows you, believe Him, and believe your wife while offering her an apology and create boundaries for all the other women you may minister to as a pastor or leader. Invite your wife with you during ministry sessions. We are better when we partner together in healthy life-giving relationships with our spouses and one another. We were wired for community. To God, be the glory! It's not all in your head.

Vicki Hart is an author, speaker, wife, mother of two married children, and Mimi to three grandchildren. She served with her husband for over 30 years in pastoral ministry, managed a successful real estate business, worked as an office manager, and is currently a Certified Professional Life Coach. She is also a Certified DISC (Personality) Consultant. Vicki is passionate about empowering women to grow in their faith, discover their strengths, passions, and desires and then to become their own unique masterpiece. She truly believes that women are stronger together. She is currently enrolled in Healing Care Ministries' Two Year Spiritual Direction program to grow and gain further tools to inspire and equip others on their spiritual journey. As an Enneagram Type 9w8 (The Advisor), she is adventurous, empathetic, perceptive, and insightful to bring out the speck of gold in others. She loves to challenge others to be the very best that God created them to be.

The purpose of this book is first and foremost to let women know that their voice and insight matter. Secondly, it is to strengthen marriages and bring awareness of the issue of transference in the church. If you are wondering what transference is and why pastors, in particular, are extremely susceptible then you simply must read this book. Strong marriages build a legacy for generations to come. Lastly, by sharing with you a painful and difficult chapter in her life and how she got to the other side perhaps others might be inspired to press on through a difficult season of their own. The theme for this book then would be hope. Hope is needed now in our world more than ever. There is nothing more powerful to move us forward into the abundant life that Jesus promised.

CPSIA information can be obtained
at www.ICGtesting.com
Printed in the USA
DVHW042238171220
595904BV00017B/477